At the fair.

1

At the fair we went
on the ferris wheel.
It was fun but mom
was scared.

At the fair we went
on the roller coaster.
It was fun but dad
was scared.

At the fair we went
on the octopus.
It was fun but baby
brother was scared.

4

At the fair we went
on the flying chair.
It was fun but
granny was scared.

At the fair we went on the bumper cars. It was fun but uncle was scared.

At the fair we went
on the water slide.
It was fun but big
brother was scared.

At the fair we went
on the ghost train.
It was fun but
I was scared.